I0211778

peasant

"'In the catalog of our errata,' Annie Woodford writes, 'record this survival.' Her new book embodies its own command, recording human and more-than-human acts of survival in an era of climate crisis. Woodford evokes the histories of the region we now call Appalachia in wise, intimate poems that offer up the resilience of its people and ecosystems as well as the racist and classist past and present of the United States. *Peasant* reveals deeply human efforts to persist in a deeply beloved landscape."

ANNA LENA PHILLIPS BELL
AUTHOR OF *ORNAMENT* AND EDITOR OF *ECOTONE*

peasant

ANNIE WOODFORD

PULLEY
PRESS

©2025 Annie Woodford

All rights reserved. Printed in the United States of America. Except as permitted
under the United States Copyright Act of 1976, no part of this publication may be
reproduced or distributed in any form or by any means, or stored in a database or
retrieval system, without the prior written permission of the publisher.

ISBN 979-8-9990158-1-5

Cover and book design by Thomas Eykemans
Cover art by Alison Hall, "A Ballad (a goddamn broken-heart, from beauty)" (2022)

Published by Pulley Press
Pulley Press is a nonprofit that promotes and celebrates rural poets and poetry.
Learn more at www.pulleypress.com

for Marion and her little Ariel

Contents

III

IV

peasant food . . . must be mixed with your hands.
Grandmother taught us that.

Nikki Giovanni

I

the fact is the falling.
the dream is the tree.

Lucille Clifton

A Poem for Puss in Boots and Marina Tsvetaeva

This is an old story,
my grandmother's favorite:

the miller's son must strip naked
out of his poor clothes to be reborn.

Puss's first gift to the king is a bag of grouse.
His next a warm nest of rabbits.

His boots gleam. His whiskers twitch
while sunlight makes the coloring book calavera

I taped to my windowpane bare
its teeth, colored in by my child's eager

hand, each mark deep, each mark hard:
the reddest red, the blue made black

by pushing the marker back and forth
across the paper until a hole

purls up from the surface. Sugar:
I place it on your tongue, my reader.

Sugar: grind the grit with your teeth.
Winter makes us all old in the end.

Dying is not beautiful.
You must trick the king.

Old Christmas

"Old Christmas" is an Appalachian tradition of celebrating
Christmas according to the Julian Calendar

The claw, the craw, the red-
tailed hawk, dusk-wise,
roosting in a bare catalpa tree.
Harsh old mountains in January.
Matted grass. The body flayed
open like a milkweed pod.
The body as muddy pasture.
I think I was a field once.
I think I was a cow-smudged creek.
A bull lived in me. He liked to sleep.
Herds of deer half darkness
wavered across me. In winter
I froze. In spring I bled wet-
weather branches. Water witching.
At midnight on Christmas Eve,
all the animals in me knelt—
coyote, cow, the field mice
vibrating with fear, the groundhog
somnolent with cold.
The Christ Child stirred under
my meadow grass, the circles of manure.
Half-light threaded the thin trees
edging the creek.
A warm animal exhaled.
The last stars fell, tinkling
and horrific, the sky arced,
a chest cavity filled with pain
and pooling blood, the red
flush of suffering under its skin.

Standing in Front of Anselm Kiefer's
Landscape with Wing
*At the Virginia Museum of Fine Arts, located beside
the headquarters of The Daughters of the Confederacy*

Dark furrows marked
by mud-stuck straw lead
the eye up to the sliver
of sky nearly pressed
out of the frame
of this massive
painting, the primal land-
scape tipped up toward
the spring's feeble sun
and all the blood spilled
on farmland and field
plowed under
the cold and fallow
earth. An angel wing
strung on wires hangs
above the dirt,
a mechanism
of lead, an echo
of old battles.
The land remembers:
a child is crying.
An ancestor digs a hole
to hold a pregnant woman's
belly while she is whipped.
Gold is pulled from teeth.
An uncle disappears.

The body of a boy
beaten to death
is weighted down
with a cotton-gin fan.
Perhaps angels are
that heavy.

Forest Primer

Debris. Detritus. Leaves releasing tannin, heat, decay.
A centipede flows over, under, over, under the rain-
darkened intricacy of the forest floor, yellow stripe
& moving legs mimicking stippled, scattered sunlight.
A deer wheels away from me, cantaloupe & brown,
dapple-traces fading, softened by the end of summer,
briar-snagged & barb wire scarred. Tick spotted. Thin
& resilient, haunches muscle-stripped, huffing at me then,
from a distance, breathing in all scent & information
(*It wanted you to move*, my father said later).
        I was reading Turgenev in the woods—
Sketches from a Hunter's Album—the short night
in the country. The heat. The open air, the river, the cover.
The springhead. Waiting in starlight or dawn-light. Ashes
blown off potatoes taken from the coals. There is the narrator
but also the two levels of peasant narrative—
one for the aristocrats & one between each other,
which they keep hidden from everyone except each other
—Grief & desire. Poverty & poetry. Poultry. Feathers
stuck to warm brown eggs. How much a rood of timber
is really worth. Where the deer bed down.

Why the Sea is Salt

I should take a vow
of silence hold my
words swear not to spell
out all the worries
worst-case-scenarios
what needs not be said
put the dog back on the leash
take the guns out of the house
unravel my mother's addiction
to cigarettes follow the red yarn
all the way back to the source my mama
walking to the store for her big sisters
who pay her in Winstons
keep the helmet on my niece's
shining brow unsmash
the beloved's face
undrink the whiskey
unhinge that trapdoor
in the sky
crows are flying out
and they are hungry
they are laughing

What I've Found Along the Zionville Road

A muddy slip
hung over a tree branch
by its champagne lace.

A cracked plastic urn
from Charlotte Crematorium.
Dirty diapers

melon-fat with rain.
White Claw cans.
A copperhead inside a tire.

Over fifty whippets canisters
in Carolina Blue.
A nest of orange-tipped

syringes almost hidden
by the deep green groundcover
leading down to the creek

paralleling this road,
the backway
between two counties.

More than one mattress
assimilating into undergrowth.
Couches. Plastic storage tubs.

Garbage bags spilling
household trash—
McDonalds wrappers,

Styrofoam peanuts, empty two liters.
A waterbed blackened by mold,
draped over a massive boulder.

A cellophane produce bag
for Cotton Candy grapes.
Chic-fil-A containers.

A gleam of muddy road
glazed with melting snow.
A curious horse rising

to meet me, white blaze
crossing his wide brow.
A tawny stone

I mistook for a coyote.
And every so often
a spring seeping

out of the bank
above me, stones
slick with water.

1.5°C

—the global temperature rise limit required to prevent large-scale suffering, according to the Intergovernmental Panel on Climate Change

We've been dreaming

our own demise
for too long now,

but my girl?

She searches
the internet
for inspirational sayings.

She asks
how much
college costs.

She stands on her toes,
to see how close
we are in height

& imagines the forest

before the hemlocks died,

before the chainsaw

found it, before

temperature shifts
& weed killers

silenced the insects

silenced the birds.

    What will our daughters do
with all this rain,

        all that fracked
water flooding the Gulf?

How long before
        the tipping point?

Is the future
a burning throat?

A boat with no home?

A hemlock dead

        to the crown?

        To be
hungry,

     to live

underground—

        bombs
falling on bombed-out
houses—

        has always
been present tense

but in America we are
still brutally innocent.

The power flickers
& then stays
off.

Jack's House

an ars poetica written after learning that the home of Ray Hicks, legendary Appalachian Storyteller and keeper of the Jack Tales, was burned down in a fire started by an arsonist

   August is skin-feel & pant,
an idyll in the arms
of the grain wife, the green wife,
   growing dry & golden in the heat.
The steep pastures the limestone allows,
however, are blanketed by the cool air
   that flows from the mountain
where the storyteller lived,
in a house that's since burned down.
   Two sides of his porch were walled up
with intricate stacks of kindling
& I don't know much about how to tell stories
   or how to start fires, how to keep fires going
in a woodstove blacked last spring to a shine
but I can still conjure woods turning
   dark in the dusk, a window candled
from the inside floating
on cricket song & turkey call.
   I can still knock on that cabin door.

Soft, Softer

A mess of rabbits, a mess
of squirrels. I remember
their tiny bones, their falling-
off flesh stewed in gravy.
Sop it up with light bread,
a salty thin savor tasting
of the can of Bunker Hill
beef my granny would mix
with it and the quick heartbeat
in the trees, the tremor,
the brown fur, the pasture
at dusk, the skin ripped off
the meat, neat slice at the anus,
a bouquet of squirrel tails
thrown to the dogs and what I wanted
most of all when I was a child
was a rabbit-skin coat,
to wear their soft wealth
to school, a clover-fed abundance,
the closest I could get
to the miracle of small mammals
I could touch as much as I wanted.

II

what I
wanted was what there was, Earth a
                    ball of
dust and water. . .

Nathaniel Mackey

there is no new water in this world

        the rain said try

to imagine me

      falling

through you

the black mud

your blood

became

        the slivers

that remain

of your once electric brain

because right now you are

becoming

     closer

to your awareness   of how

I press your cold wet coat

to your skin

you don't have to leave behind

the gift

of feeling

more delight than discomfort

you can   swim

After Alison Hall's *Field Guide*

"hands behind hands" —*Thomas Hardy*

This ministry of bones, pencil marks   fragile & flawed: you can see the quiver in the hand.

The soft lead spreads, rock that it is, back   to the first scraped line. Stars fall across altar boards.

They become stitches against death, reinforcing the fact of death. The artist makes her devotions over & over:

we must pray without ceasing. Endearment of plaster, of rabbit skin glue, binding agent boiled down,

a protein derived from grass, from the chase, the heart   beating fast. These wooden frames were built by

men who learn early on not to show what they feel. Daddy was a craftsman too & his daddy before that.

Hand-rubbed: dust & heat building up, blown away by human breath, pluming out & down—inhaled.

Two generations ago, these hands   would have thumbed the first yellow seedlings of spring,

threaded a weft, pieced scraps of fabric together to keep babies & old folks alive.

Her grandmother tatted a bedspread big enough for a marriage bed or to wrap a body in.

And it's trick of history   these hands   now measure the space between Giotto's stars.

The meditations of dead relatives   (*sharecropper, loom watcher*)   culminate in chapel art.

In a cold room in Germany, Piedmont sky   (*Southside, Bright Leaf*) throws its light into the world.

Her touch is sometimes tremulous.   These are carpenter marks.

All Strange Wonders

for Ann More, wife of John Donne, who died in childbirth

I kept my fingers stained
　　with walnuts, paint, pencil lead, my garden,
India Ink trying to teach myself calligraphy.
　　My hands brushed over the grass,
my brow, across the narrow backs of my children,
pages of books now foxed and brittle.
　　　　My nails are no longer busy
　　　　catching dirt and being cleaned of dirt,
my hands are no longer instruments of doing.
Maybe I'm the stirring
　　of wind through woods that rise
above you, the winter-shiver
of beech leaves sun-faded and singing
　　　　about all kinds of falling.

An Aunt Story, Improvised as a Blues Line

She was the widow-bone,
the insistence
        of the womb
ever since a boy laid her
down in a cold attic room,
the stick of feather ticking
part of her pleasure.
She kept her eyes downcast
at the Army Navy
where, once a year,
her husband paid cash
for three pairs of little shoes.
She stirred
        the powder, yellow
as marigolds, into the olio,
and kept a small covered
dish of fatback for him
on the counter.
          She saved
her strangest songs,
the ones she'd always
known, for the babies,
keeping time in a creaking
ladder back chair
        I still have.
So when he was shot
in the gut for being a bully,
for slapping strangers
across the back with the stick
he kept behind the bar

of his poolhall,
for laughing as he pointed
the long black barrel
of his shotgun at their heads,
the violence was   not
shocking but felt like part
of the nature of this place,
where the long knives
were usually out,
where the women stand
and wait.   That much
was true   and she knew it.
So there was not much
mourning and her children
she took to her parents,
to the house
             in the mountains
rich hippies would   one day
own, the house
with the fireplace
big enough for a child
to stand in, where her father
             would be
remembered for his beatings,   her mother
already half-blind with sugar.
She went on the knitting line,
running a   sewing machine
until she became a needle
herself,   punching
up and down for the half
a paycheck she didn't send
her children and a man
she lived with who had

a cough, but who knew
the old songs   and some
of the new—Muleskinner, New
River Freightrain,
Shaking. Shaking
that sugar down.
And when she felt
that knot and when she felt
it get bigger, she stopped
letting him touch her
stomach,   stopped
eating all but crackers
and instant coffee.
A strip of wallpaper
          bubbled up
in her room.
          She watched it.
One time her son came to stay.
She helped him make
a history project, cutting
pictures out of old
National Geographics,
slicing   through
the paper just above
          a brown breast
on the other side
of a dugout canoe
            they glued down.
          When she died
in the old hospital,
she was in the women's ward,
her bed surrounded by curtains
and the calls of other patients.

Her children came
and stood around her,
but no one stayed
        while her tumor
carried her away,
        big as her babies
once were and pressing
up against her lungs, until,
filled with fluid,
    she could no longer breathe.
She was something
like a bunch of mistletoe
shot down   from a tree.

White Pines: And I Shiver
the Whole Night Through

Feathers of green flame
the undergrowth,

needles of young trees
with trunks like wrists,

breathing in this clearest
of sun-sharp days.

A brilliance of sap must lift,
square cells converting star-matter

and solar flare into chlorophyll.
I used to fuck and fight

and feel life alight
within me just to tear it out.

Now I live in a body
heavy with blunted lust

and love made fearful
by loss. I am walking

through the shattered
light on these pines.

I am remembering my dead
and my own death and the death

that will come for those I love,
disturbing cowbirds in stolen nests.

And they rise up, quiet
except for wings.

Many Steeples Would Have to Be Stacked One on Top of Another to Reach from the Bottom to the Surface of the Sea

The Little Mermaid Speaks

baby-tide
death-tide
the clean mouths
of newborns
the clean bones
a tossed prophesy
of swallow
& purge
seabirds
my father's swollen feet
my swollen feet
doomsday
bloomsday
i can still feel
my father's hands
pulling my hair
into a rough ponytail
my skin held
the smell of fish
even in the prince's
antechamber
i was voiceless
each step a stab
the nether
regions reached

by salt
yaupon tea
as cure-all
a nutria
with a snake
in its mouth
trots through me
a doe crashes
across this estuary
in the rain
whole cloth
sail cloth
the briny expanse
o swim in it
certain waters
i love foam
of souls & wave-
turn cockleshells
& silverbells
an acre of land
between the salt
water & the sea
sand i was
a little girl
peering through
a porthole
untangling
silver minnows
from a throw net

Soon the Red Wolf

will be but genetic code
stored in metal drawers.
Hunted in pocosin swamps,
within the Weyerhaeuser stands,
that crop of pulp drained & dried to tinder,

come spring the half-coyote pups will be

snout deep in warm fawn meat—
wolf-tall, rough coats burnished
by a touch of rust, bellies gorged with blood,
breathing in the fine mist of fungicide
sprayed by machines that crawl the loblollies:

in the catalog of our errata, record this survival.

III

America,
you are my teeth,
rotting even as I live

. . . .

but I will gum you
till I die

Jim Webb

A Long Line of Hard and Angry Women:
A Summoning

All our grandmothers and aunts and second cousins
once removed gather around us,
tough jawed and bent upon survival,

they of the tombstone set into the side of a hill,
of the anonymous corporate cemetery,
of the rock half hidden by leaves.

Of the family plot upended by roots.
Womb to womb I conjure
your bleach and lye-bitten hands.

Wilkes County Posada

Come winter solstice
the Tyson Chicken Plant will turn
golden, the turning lifting

safety signs, hiring bonus signs,
the refrigerated trucks waiting to pull away.
The puddles of nameless muck.

The narrow smokestack spilling white steam.
The fathers who come home
smelling of blood and chicken funk.

The pear trees planted along the street
will turn crimson, turn purple.
O county of many poultry houses

and children who believe
in the FFA, white feathers fly
out of stacked cages, the birds inside them

unable to stand. Somewhere tonight a mother
is pulling on steel-toed boots
and taping up the cuts on her hands.

She's planning Christmas
with every naked bird she disassembles,
with every wing cut free

from the body, with every body
wrapped in plastic.
Somewhere outside of town tonight,

perhaps where the old racetrack buckles
as frost falls and thaws,
where fields of winter wheat flow,

the Christ Child is being
reassembled, continually reassembled,
mortal rib by mortal rib.

He wears a onesie from Walmart.
His mama works the nightshift,
so he stays with his grandma,

whose hands—curled up
from a lifetime of repetitive labor—
trace a bumblebee's flight

toward his laughing belly.
And the cold gathers around us
like the three wisemen.

And the chickens are kneeling in the slaughterhouse,
the cows are kneeling in the field.
And space heaters sometimes short out.

And trailers are built of many flammable materials.
Fighter jets from Fort Bragg
make practice runs over us.

The terrible stars sometimes fall,
but we are asleep in the valley,
we are asleep in each other's arms.

The Country

In the cleft of red-
brown land, two long rows
of potato plants are white
with Sevin Dust,
the Appalachians above
a green wall making their own mist.
I can imagine my neighbor
shaking that powder over their leaves
from the toe of an old pair of pantyhose
(a favorite of the old folks
and one I know
I breathed in as a child).

Lining It Out

when you see a crow
it's liable to have lived
nearby for years

clatter of wings above buckshot

my father the crow-shooter
I must own

Wild Strawberries

for your grandmama (after Alice Walker)

The first heat is a calling.
Wash the blue laundry.
Thread a melody

through a penny whistle—
a song of swallows,
of wash tubs, of a girl

learning how to sweep,
snipped buttons kept
in a *Hav-a-Tampa* box,

her favorite story
the one about the North Wind
blowing the bowl of grain away.

Harvest, hard times,
crowder peas & cracked crocks
held together with copper wire—

interrupt this poem
with grief. Here's a garden
draping foothills' sway,

pole beans snapped & translated
in pressure cooker steam,
meat stretched with milk gravy,

beans seasoned with bone.
Here is a repetition of scissors,
cutting thick fabric to cover

wing-back chairs,
the pattern knotting the hands,
tacks held in teeth,

varnish breathed in,
white bread sandwiches bleeding
Better Boys & German Pinks.

Chatterbox on the break room radio.
Shift work, short shrift—murmurations
in the midst of clamor.

The soul's a throng of swallows,
shape shifting against factory ceilings.
A white bird—

transient as the soap bubbles
beat to peaks, rinsed
from a child's brow,

churned in a mop bucket
before laying to worn linoleum—
calls from out a bare bush,

cleaving cold with a song,
its breast a cloud weighted with snow
& our grandmothers would say

birds bring messages.
Don't let one in the house
or take a baby from the nest—

the warble in your palm
certain to be abandoned
by its mother once you touch it.

A bedspread made
for a marriage bed,
hand-tatted by big-knuckled hands,

sweeps over all of this.
Wings of white eyelets
seine the landscape,

gather up birds & starlight,
gather up mountain ranges
still raw from the last ice age,

a name hidden
in the stem of a wild strawberry
twining the edge

of an illuminated manuscript,
eiderdown grass
your grandmother foraged as a child.

She is holding out a handful now,
a spill of small berries,
misshapen & tasting of rain.

In the Pipeline's Path

for Red Terry

Pippins and scarlet oaks, she said.

She took to her tree because she knew she'd never see any of this
      again—
the wayward field, the water meadow filled with late spring rain
filtering down to the aquifer's hidden well.
The way southeastern trees turkey-call against each other
when they rub high branches in high wind.

She lived in the whippoorwill's liquid note.

Pippen—the name for an apple that used to mean *seed*—
is an old word for a new world.

And most of the orchards are gone.

The few rows she still has she has not for money, but to know
that the animals come—black bear, deer, the careful raccoon—
to eat the windfall turning sweet in tall grass,
to leave behind scat bejeweled with seed,

tracks of paw print and claw,
rubbed bark, the bitten twig.

Here's to the Land of the Long-Leaf Pine

Wal-Mart has to keep
their diabetes supplies
in plastic, theft-proof cases,

neuropathy cream   as sacred
relic   resonating
behind scratched Lucite.

You Can Do Whatever the Hell You Want

for Robert Ryman

he was a jazz musician first
                              all ecstasy
                  is absurd all ecstasy

is obvious like this

     & nothingness becomes
something if you look
at it closely enough

layered paint fine as veils

vernix & caul   a membrane permeable

to other worlds

you can do whatever the hell you want
he seems to say   free &
religious

at the same time   the edges
of a series on squares of wood
different depending upon which side
you approach them from you want

to go nose to nose with the suspended
sheet of plyboard big as a trailer
            look at the long shimmer
              of its length no shimmer

is not the true word

rather it is like a plain

       a movement like grass

shadows move across it

there's so much heartbreak
in a white painting

one handprint
could ruin it

IV

Desire is spacious.

Airea D. Matthews

My Mother Advises Me on How to Survive February

Turn *Going To*
   into *Gone,*
as in *I'm gone*
   clean my house today.
Add the *at* at the end
   of your question
to show you know
   it's never cut and dry
Where Anything Is At.
   If you sweep
under someone's feet
   they will never marry.
Don't move a broom
   to a new house.
When visiting,
   never leave
through a new door,
   your luck wafting
with the wind
   through the house.
All the secret
   floors we stand upon
sometimes open
   like trap doors
under our feet.
   Never look a dog
you don't know
   in the eyes.

Don't make snow
    cream out of the first snow.
Don't tell your dreams
    before breakfast
or they will come true.
    Don't step on graves
(this is practical advice).
    Feel the feet of the dying
to know.
    There are some things
you just shouldn't
    think about.
Look above you
    when you see
a scratched-out place
    in the leaves
for turkeys roosting
    in the trees,
quiet and clever,
    drab like us
until they open
    their intricately patterned
other selves,
    feathers of the richest
brown edged
    with black arrows
or like snow
    cross hatched by branches,
spurred and massive,
    a flash of some force
from the woods,
    scent of duff
and bracken sky.

The Four Hundred Angels of Henry County

after Philip Levine's "On My Own"

My first cradle was the moss inside
a stump, deep in a forest
where chestnuts still grew.

The wandering cow
found me, led my father
to me & her hidden calf

& we came home
in a muddy-kneed parade,
game for the path,

game for the gate
swinging open—
tick-trefoil hitched

on my rough blanket, the cuffs
of my father's jeans,
the cow's switching tail.

I was held in the crook
of my big father's big arm.
I am told he was happier then.

I kept a swatch of that thin
K-mart flannel for a quilt
I've been meaning to make,

along with the tiny pink rosette
on the tiny pink bodice
of my mother's one bikini,

for I was a baby born on the shining
warm waters of my mother's
man-made lake, flooded

over an abandoned iron mine
& the old fires rose
through green water

& entered my veins
& though I was a lonely child,
I was also free, my mother

sleeping off third shift
on the sofa while I drew
red birds, blue birds, & robins

beside her. She'd wake
long enough to fix an awkward wing,
curl their feet around a branch

& tell me never to erase.
Dogwood blossoms grew
to full size under my crayons,

my father taking me fishing
when their petals started to fall
on the Smith or maybe I never

fished, but had the rod
handed to me just after
the rainbow struck.

A Chassis of the Creation Is Love

after Joy Priest

"& that a kelson of the creation is love"—Whitman

My cousin had a '78 gray Thunderbird with gray velvet seats &
headlights that opened & closed like jewel boxes.
My dad helped him put a 400 engine in it &
when my cousin totaled it my dad took those seats—
wide, soft, luxurious—& put them in our Rambler.
Perched on the center bench that swung out between the front
      bucket seats,
I rode in swirls of cigarette smoke and George Jones.
On long rides home, I slept stretched in the back, the stars gallop-
      ing above me.
I would tuck my fingers into the intricate upholstery & rub the
      silken nap.
Dad painted the Rambler gray & put a black double-pinstripe
      down its panel.
I got that pin-striper one time and painted wavy lines on his
      junked cars.
In later years, the seats were a low couch for his shop,
an excess amid concrete & grease, tipping back
a little when you sat on them.

A Song for the Daughters of Europa

Every time we pass that pasture
I point out the bull to my daughter,
who was never taught to know a bull

and therefore to spot one, when
needed, in a field of cows. But once
you've seen one, they will always stand out—

the massive neck, the muscled shoulders'
more dangerous than any female Angus.
I name the bull for Granny, who named them

for me and believed in the red myth
and in getting over the nearest fence
fast as you can. I know now

this was her only way, the lesson
pressed in by the little stones
of her eyes. I see the girl she must have been,

her hay-straw hair fine, like mine,
and barely holding a rag curl,
her canvas sneakers well-washed

but still stained by farmwork.
She is out in the dawn, an hour before
school, where she is the fastest

at math. She's calling down the milk
cow, the copper penny leaves
of the locust tree, her footprints left in frost.

Once she grabbed my hand
just as she grabbed the electric
fence and, when the shock passed
through her and into me, she laughed.

Draft Animal

Percherons hold their strength at bay, quivering
against the rein, metal nailed to hooves
and clamped against their mouths. Brown velvet
and sweat. They hold back and then they give—
like all good beasts of burden—with the massive
muscle of their hearts. Deep in the steepest
coves, where hemlocks bend bewitched white limbs,
such horses still haul timber on slopes
too slanted for roads, heaving logs even
the railroad missed—patrimony
of red oaks, of hickory trees, of poplars
dropping orange flowers chained to their flanks.
I would like to be a nineteen-hand mare,
and drag those crowns shaking with sky behind me.

The Last American Hero Speaks His Piece

for Junior Johnson

Look here, honey, I know the appetite
of the spirit, the appetite of the body.
But you have to tend the flesh
the way Papa tended his liquor still—
build next to a spring no water flows into
except what hemlocks give.
Distill rain and laurel shade,
the last lap of the last mountain lion
before she slipped into oblivion.
I don't believe in restrictor plates
but restrict yourself.
Build a better engine every day.
Don't take to holding your liquor.
We each of us have a burden
caused by thirst.
Keep a pot of beans on the stove.
Eat cornbread and buttermilk.
Leave that store-bought bread alone.
Get seed corn saved
in some Civil War deserter's attic.
I'll tell you a secret if you'll listen:
I was quiet not because I was tough,
though I was tough.
I was quiet because prison turned me silent.
I was alone. And so are you.
Improvise if you have to.
We love our machines
because they make us
believe we can be free.

The Source of Prayer Is Not Fear, but Delight

(from the Marina Tsvetaeva's *Moscow Diaries*)

My small brown dog
sniffs at the weeping
detritus a cattle truck
dropped, the cows
& their kin released
into umber fields,
a pleasure of black calves
in blinding grass.

I pick persimmons
off the ground,
pick dirt & gravel
out of sweet,
puckered skin.
(First frost. First frost
fell sometime last week)
I roll the meat off
the many flat seeds
with my tongue
& spit them at the sun.

Dryland Fish

This is an elegy for the memory of skin—
his wide, freckled back, the way he cut a grapefruit
for me so the fruit slipped from the pith.

Once, we went to the forest. Morels pushed up
where long gray poplars marked the richest duff,
(first skim of green on mountainsides in spring),

the thrice-logged wildness nevertheless changing
the charge in the air—rhizome, ozone, water
rising through the trees' tight grain. We lay down.

To Set Budding More, and Still More
after John Keats's "To Autumn"

September, season
of Joe Pye Weed—
soft, purple, planetary—
in a mess of briars
at the edge of fields
where hay's been laid down,
you bake silage bronze
with midday sun. Apples
fall. Unpecked muscadines
dry out, turn dusty
in the arbor's deep shade.
You flush my cheeks, flush
jakes and jennys—warbles
of wings and woodsmoke
from tree rafters—good
talismans, spurred and pattened.
We ride in the back of the truck,
up, out of the cool bottom's
green current, up through
frog call and cow gaze,
hair still wet from the creek,
shivering as the large body
of Firescale Mountain darkens.
We ride into katydids,
poplars soughing off sun.
As you stand against the cab,
we discuss how to name the way
sorghum holds your red heat in dusk,

lining out old songs in its stalks—
the *heads*, the *blossoms*,
the *tassels*, we say.

Loving-kindness

Start with place names
in Western North Carolina—

Boomer, Level Cross,
Shacktown, Traphill,
Vashti, Vilas,
Devotion, Harmony,
Love Valley, Hiddenite
Ennice, Cricket,
Ronda.

Send them to your brother,
who would understand
their delight, though
he drives by your house
but does not stop.

Let them be a map
on the way to agape.

Forest Prayer

O Lord let me lose myself
to the dense net of leaves—
witch hazel, laurel, all the shimmering
pin pricks of white pine—
like a black bear burrowed
under an overhanging rock
covered in running cedar & red-capped lichen,
in a room of packed dirt & roots polished
by the oil in my fur, a den running deep into the hillside,
a place a person would walk right over
& not realize was there.
Let me be the stillness listening
in green shade, attuned
to the descent of poplar flowers
falling all around me,
my ever-seeing snout pressed first to the earth
& then lifted to catch scent after scent
flowing over this mountain—
crushed pine and cut sap, car exhaust,
honeycomb, grublight,
my small eyes easily mistaken
for a skitter of sun in the woods.
Let me find a stand of mayapples
on some south-facing slope
to roll in, their sharp-tongued blossoms,
my mouth watering for their hard sour fruit.
Let me crush the juice out of their stems
& dig newborn voles—thin-skinned and pink—
out from under the wide fragrant body of a fallen hemlock.
Let me give birth in my sleep.

Let me spend all winter in a tender half-dream.
Let me live always as something warm
& alive moving through the trees,
giving shape to the shadow.

Acknowledgments

The poet is grateful that some of the poems in this manuscript
have appeared or will appear in the following publications:

Appalachian Journal
Asheville Poetry Review
Bear Review
Beloit Poetry Journal
Crossing the Rift: North Carolina Poets on 9/11 & Its Aftermath, Press 53
Cutleaf Journal
Gulf Coast (online)
Bull City Press' Inch microchapbook series
Michigan Quarterly Review's Mixtape
North Carolina Literary Review
Raleigh Review
Rattle Poem of the Week
Salvation South
Smartish Pace
Southern Humanities Review
Southern Poetry Anthology Volume III: Contemporary Appalachia
Southern Poetry Review

I am forever grateful to the community I have found at the Appalachian Writers' Workshop.

Thank you to Alison Hall, my oldest and dearest friend, for your generous artistic spirit in my life.

Thank you to Alison Romano for your exquisite attention to my books over the years.

Thank you to Andy Fogle and Cameron MacKenzie for being such attentive readers of my work and for engaging me in conversations about poetry that brought joy and revelation to my work. Thank you to *Salvation South* and *Blackbird* for publishing those conversations.

Thank you also to the North Carolina Writers' Network for the many events and workshops that inspired me as I wrote this book.

Note:

The line "the long knives/were usually out" in "An Aunt Story, Improvised as a Blues Line" comes from a quote in Beth Macy's *Factory Man* by Spencer Morten, grandson-in-law of J.D. Bassett, founder of Bassett Furniture Company: "They used to say of Mr. J.D., 'The old fool dyes his hair.' People in Bassett were tough. The long knives were usually out."

About the Author

Annie Woodford studied poetry at Hollins College and teaches at Wilkes Community College in North Carolina. She is the author of *Bootleg* (Groundhog Poetry Press, 2019) and *Where You Come from Is Gone* (Mercer UP, 2022), which was awarded the 2022 Weatherford Award for Appalachian Poetry. Her micro-chapbook, *When God Was a Child*, was published by Bull City Press in 2023. She has been the recipient of the Jean Ritchie Fellowship, the Thelma Smallwood Scholarship at the Appalachian Writers' Workshop, and the Guy Owen Prize by *Southern Poetry Review*. She has also been a Rona Jaffe Poetry Scholar at Bread Loaf and a Tennessee Williams Scholar at the Sewanee Writers' Conference. In 2023, she was the writer-in-residence at Radford University's Highland Summer Conference.

www.ingramcontent.com/pod-product-compliance
Lightning Source LLC
Chambersburg PA
CBHW020215090426
42734CB00008B/1081